Big Freeze

Catherine Chambers

Heinemann Library
Chicago, Illinois

Designed by Visual Image
Illustration by Paul Bale
Originated by Ambassador Litho
Printed and bound in South China

06 05 04 03 02
10 9 8 7 6 5 4 3 2 1

Library of Congress Cataloging-in-Publication Data
Chambers, Catherine, 1954-
  Big freeze / Catherine Chambers.
      p. cm. -- (Wild weather)
Summary: Introduces what a "big freeze" is, and how some humans, plants,
and animals have adapted to living in places where these fierce ice
storms are common.
Includes bibliographical references and index.
  ISBN 1-58810-658-6 (HC), 1-4034-0109-8 (Pbk)
  1. Freezes (Meteorology)--Juvenile literature. 2. Freezes
(Meteorology)--Physiological effect--Juvenile literature. [1. Freezes
(Meteorology)] I. Title. II. Series.
  QC905 .C48 2002
  551.5'253--dc21
                             2002000816

Acknowledgments
The author and publishers are grateful to the following for permission to reproduce copyright material: pp. 4, 12, 13, 14,
28 Photodisc; pp. 5, 11, 16, 17, 22, 24, 29 Corbis; p. 6 Robert Harding Picture Library; pp. 7, 18, 21, 25 Stone; p. 9
Telegraph Colour Library; p. 15 Imagebank; p. 19 Ardea; pp. 20, 23 Reuters; p. 26 Associated Press; p. 27 Bryan and
Cherry Alexander.

Cover photograph: Ric Ferro/Black Star Publishing/PictureQuest.

Every effort has been made to contact copyright holders of any material reproduced in this book. Any omissions will be
rectified in subsequent printings if notice is given to the publisher.

Some words are shown in bold, **like this.** You can
find out what they mean by looking in the glossary.

Contents

What Is a Big Freeze?

Some places on Earth are cold all year round. Others are warm all year round. Most places are cool in winter and warm in the summer.

Winter is usually about the same **temperature** every year. Sometimes it gets much colder than normal, even for winter. Rivers, lakes, and the ground may **freeze.** This is called a big freeze.

Where Do Big Freezes Happen?

The areas around the **North** and **South Poles** are cold all the time. Winter weather is normal there. It is not a big **freeze.**

Florida is usually warm for most of the year.
When it suddenly gets cold there, people, plants,
and animals may not be ready. They can be
harmed by the cold. This is a big freeze.

What Makes it So Cold?

In places far from the **Equator,** the Sun's rays are spread over a wider area. This makes the Sun's warmth weaker. In winter, these places **tilt** away from the Sun. The air and ground get very cold.

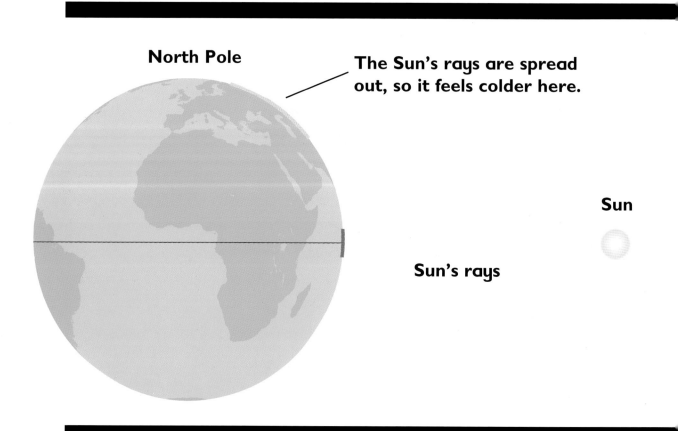

North Pole

The Sun's rays are spread out, so it feels colder here.

Sun

Sun's rays

Days are shorter during the winter, so the Sun has less time to warm the Earth. The heat in the ground rises high above the Earth.

Why Do Big Freezes Happen?

There are moving **masses** of air all around the Earth. Some are warm and some are cold. A big **freeze** happens when a mass of cold air stays in one place for a long time.

These masses of cold air often come from around the **North** and **South Poles**, where it is cold all year round. Strong winds push the cold air to other places, bringing them a big freeze.

What Are Big Freezes Like?

In a big **freeze,** the weather is even colder than normal winter weather. Some big freezes are so cold that it is dangerous to stay outside for too long. They can last for a few days or a few weeks.

Sometimes ice and snow fall during a big
freeze. This can make the roads and sidewalks
very slippery. But in many big freezes the skies
are clear. It is too cold to snow.

Harmful Freezes

It can be hard to travel in a big **freeze.** Ice can make roads slippery. Water freezes around boats so that they cannot move.

If it gets very cold, water can freeze inside water pipes. When water freezes, it **expands.** It can crack the pipes. When the big freeze **thaws,** the water gushes out and causes **floods.**

Big Freeze in Mongolia

Mongolia, in Asia, is located in the middle of the **continent.** It gets very hot in the summer and very cold in the winter. Breezes from the sea cannot reach the middle of the continent.

Many people in Mongolia are farmers or
herders. In one big **freeze** many cows and
sheep died. They died because there was nothing
to eat. All the grass was frozen.

Preparing for a Big Freeze

Some people buy extra food before a big **freeze** comes. They will not have to go outside to go shopping. Hospitals and drugstores order plenty of extra medicines.

A big freeze can kill **crops.** So farmers often
cover plants with **fleece,** foam, or glass. They
use heaters and wind machines to blow warm
air onto fruit trees.

Coping with Big Freezes

When it is very cold, it is important to dress warmly. Wearing several layers of clothing under your coat will help keep you warm. Mittens, hats, and boots are important too.

It is best to stay inside during a big **freeze.**
Getting enough to eat helps your body to stay
warm. Hot food and drinks are a tasty way to
beat a big freeze!

A Big Freeze in a Hot Country

India and Bangladesh are normally very hot countries. People wear clothes that help them to keep cool in the hot weather. Their houses are not built to keep them warm.

In 2001, the weather in these countries was much colder than usual. Many people died because their clothes and houses could not protect them from the **freezing** weather.

Animals and Plants in a Big Freeze

Some animals that live in cold places, like these yaks, have thick fur that keeps them warm. Other animals are not used to such cold weather. It is a good idea to keep your pets inside during a big **freeze.**

If a big freeze comes too early in the year, it can damage **crops.** Frost makes plants freeze and can keep them from growing. These strawberry plants are covered in ice.

To the Rescue!

Cities in warm parts of the world may not have enough snowplows and salt trucks to cope with a big **freeze.** They may have to borrow trucks from colder places.

Siberia in Russia gets very cold in the winter. In 2001 it was even colder than usual, and ice blocked the Lena River. Planes dropped bombs on the thick ice to keep the river from **flooding.**

Adapting to Big Freezes

If you live in a home with central heating or a fireplace, it is easy to stay warm when a big **freeze** comes. Sometimes people put plastic over their windows to keep the cold out.

In many cities there are people without homes.
They sleep outside on the street. For homeless
people, a big freeze can be dangerous. It is
important that they find food and **shelter.**

Fact File

◆ Ice on rivers and lakes is made of millions of frozen **crystals.** The crystals join together to make the ice look smooth.

◆ The coldest **temperature** ever recorded on Earth was in Vostok, Antarctica, on July 21, 1983. It got down to -129°F (-89°C) that day!

◆ When it is windy, it often feels colder than the temperature on a **thermometer.** Scientists have developed a measurement called wind chill. It combines the temperature and the wind speed to tell you how cold it feels.

Glossary

continent huge mass of land, such as Africa

crop plant that is grown for food

crystal small shape of frozen water

Equator imaginary line around the center of the Earth. It is usually warm there.

expand to get bigger

fleece warm, furry material

flood overflow of water onto a place that is usually dry

freeze to get very cold; or, a period of very cold weather

herder someone who keeps animals for a living

mass large amount of something like air that does not have a definite shape

North Pole most northern place on Earth. It is very cold there.

shelter safe, warm place

South Pole most southern place on Earth. It is very cold there.

temperature measure of how hot or cold it is

thaw to melt

thermometer tool that is used for measuring temperature

tilt to tip slightly to one side

More Books to Read

Ashwell, Miranda, and Andy Owen. *Snow*. Chicago: Heinemann Library, 1999.

Chambers, Catherine. *Blizzard*. Chicago: Heinemann Library, 2002.

Royston, Angela. *Hot and Cold*. Chicago: Heinemann Library, 2001.

Index